Baltimore
Girl

Baltimore Girl

MARLENE PATTON

BALTIMORE GIRL

iUniverse books may be ordered through booksellers or by contacting:

iUniverse
1663 Liberty Drive
Bloomington, IN 47403
www.iuniverse.com
844-349-9409

Because of the dynamic nature of the Internet, any web addresses or links contained in this book may have changed since publication and may no longer be valid. The views expressed in this work are solely those of the author and do not necessarily reflect the views of the publisher, and the publisher hereby disclaims any responsibility for them.

Any people depicted in stock imagery provided by Getty Images are models, and such images are being used for illustrative purposes only.
Certain stock imagery © Getty Images.

ISBN: 978-1-6632-3133-8 (sc)
ISBN: 978-1-6632-3134-5 (hc)
ISBN: 978-1-6632-3135-2 (e)

Library of Congress Control Number: 2022907859

Print information available on the last page.

iUniverse rev. date: 04/23/2022

Contents

In the Beginning

By all reliable accounts, I was born on January 1, 1940, fourteen minutes after midnight. I failed to qualify as the first born that year in Baltimore, Maryland, as some little wretch of a boy beat me out by seven minutes. However, my parents got a consolation prize from the *Baltimore Sun* newspaper of sixteen shares of Standard Oil stock, a year of diaper service, and a playpen. Not bad for second place.

My parents were Louis and Amelia Herman. My father's parents were immigrants from the Rhineland who died before I was born. My mother was an Eckert, the daughter of Maggie and David. Grandfather Eckert used to sit me on a chair and braid my hair. He was a cooper by trade but died when I was five years old. Maggie was a different story; she was the most effective disciplinarian of my childhood.

The other members of the Eckert family included Uncle Fred, a Lutheran pastor who had a doctorate in theology. He was married to Aunt Dorothy, valedictorian of her college class. There was Uncle Gus, who worked in the post office. Then there were the fraternal twin girls, my mother and Aunt Catherine. After them were Uncle

Bill and his wife Aunt Marie. Uncle Bill was my favorite. He did his best to spoil me, always happy to take me out for ice cream, buy me presents, and visit when I was sick in bed.

I was an only child, some might think a rather spoiled one by parents, aunts, and uncles, but my mother and Grandma Maggie did their best to remind me of my manners and duties. When I would disappoint Grandma, she would sit me on her lap and kiss my forehead. She would then say, "You know I love you, but I am very disappointed in you." That invariably brought a spate of tears from me with promises to do better. I hated to disappoint her.

One memorable incident became a family legend. I was about five years old, and my mother was working in the kitchen. I wanted her to do something with me, but she said she was too busy and I should go to the living room and read my books. I protested and she repeated her insistence. I turned on my heels and marched away like a little Nazi but turned around and, arms akimbo, said "Buttonhole!"

She had to keep from laughing but recognized this defiance could not be tolerated, so she said, "Come back here. What did you call your mother?"

I knew I was in trouble and meekly said, "Buttonhole."

It seemed to me, to be a swear word. She said, "Don't ever speak to your mother like that again, and when Daddy comes home I'm going to tell him." That was the ultimate threat. I think they had a good laugh, and the story provided amusement for my family for years.

I don't think my childhood behavior was particularly bad, but it did occasionally get me in trouble. Like the time I went to visit Grandma around Christmas time. Earlier, I had told Santa I wanted a dollhouse. That day, I asked Grandma if I may go to the bathroom upstairs, and she said, "Fine, but don't go into Uncle Gus's room." I went upstairs and the door to his room was closed. I couldn't resist the temptation, so I quietly opened the door and there, to my wonder, was the dollhouse! I was marveling at the sight, when I heard an *ahem* and there was Grandma standing in the door. After the tears and the usual admonition, she said, "You mustn't tell your cousin Dorothy about this, because Santa asked Uncle Gus to deliver this for him." I promised but was sad that Dorothy was getting my preferred Christmas present.

On Christmas Day, I came down and there was my dollhouse! I clapped my hands and said, "It's just like Dorothy's."

Growing Up

G rowing up, we lived in Dundalk, a part of Baltimore County. It was a blue-collar neighborhood where many of the people worked for Bethlehem Steel on Sparrows Point. Our house was on Fairway, with Fairway Park across the street. The other side of the park was called Keyway Park, along Keyway, which was where my Grandma lived. It was just a short walk from our house to hers, which made it easy for me to pop in. The houses on both streets were row houses with front porches. The garages were on alleys behind the houses. In the summertime, people sat on their porches and chatted with neighbors and passersby. It was a nice place to grow up.

Dad worked at Seagram's, across town at Calvert Distillery, which is in Arbutus, on the other side of Baltimore. That meant he had an hour commute each way, at least until the Harbor Tunnel was built. He was tall, slim, and quite athletic. He could have been a professional baseball player, and was scouted by a major league team, but an accident resulted in him losing two toes, thereby ending that possible career. Mother was five foot six with blond hair and beautiful blue eyes, which I still envy. Dad had a temper, as did

Grandma Eckert, so it is a wonder that I turned out so well. (I hear a hollow laugh from my husband.)

My Aunt Catherine suffered an unfortunate accident as a child, which left her mentally disabled. Her mind was left at about a seven or eight-year-old's level. She lived with Grandma and was helpful doing chores and could converse with family. She adored me and would ask for me when ill or disturbed. We would go shopping together and I could persuade her to step on the escalator with me. In later years, after Grandma's death, she went to live in the National Lutheran Home in Rockville with Grandma's sister. There she learned to knit and help other residents, which makes me think we had underestimated her abilities.

I entered Dundalk Elementary School at age five. I was intimidated by the teacher, but blossomed as a student after that year. I would walk to school with my friend, Helen Wolinski. Mother would walk me to her house where Mrs. Wolinski, who I called Aunt Cass, would be braiding Helen's hair as she sat on a ladder-backed chair.

I can't say I liked Junior High or High School. I just didn't care for my classmates. My friends growing up went to Catholic schools, and I envied them. I went to the proms and football games at my school, but I didn't care for them.

I became an entrepreneur at age sixteen, when I put an ad in the local paper stating that I would decorate homes for Christmas. I didn't tell my parents about this venture until I showed them the ad. My father was annoyed and said that this was a waste of money because nobody would hire me. He had no sooner finished his lecture when the phone rang, a call from my first customer. Father said he would take me to the home and go to the door with me to make sure the customer was acceptable. Bless him, he did. I had a steady stream of customers for every weekday evening and Saturdays. I was paid in cash, and then put the money in an empty cigar box. I didn't count it until Christmas Eve and was delighted to report that I had earned $365. (In today's dollars that would be about $3,500!) Dad couldn't believe it, so he counted the money himself.

That same year, I went with my friend, Janice McDaniel, to visit her grandparents in Monroe, Louisiana. Mr. and Mrs. McDaniel lived on a dairy farm, and it was my first experience visiting a farm. My mother had told me not to sit around but to help out. The first morning, when it was still dark out, I got dressed and went downstairs to ask Mrs. McDaniel what I could do to help. She said I could go to the henhouse and gather the eggs. "It's the building down there with the light on."

I went there and the hens were all sitting on their eggs. When I tried to take the eggs, they pecked at me. I stood there for some time wondering what to do, when I heard Mr. McDaniel give an *ahem*. I told him I was sent to get the eggs but the chickens didn't want to give them to me. He said, "I'll show you how." He just knocked a hen off the nest and put the eggs in my basket.

I said, "But they are still warm!"

He said, "Yes, but Mrs. McDaniel will know what to do with them."

We went to church on Sunday, and at the end of the service Mr. McDaniel stood up and announced that everybody was invited to the farm for a barbecue on Saturday night. Then he said, "Fred, bring any of the boys that would like barbecue." Fred was the manager of the NY Yankees AAA farm team, located in Monroe. Most of the "boys" turned up on Saturday night. Included among them were Mickey Mantle's younger twin brothers, Roy and Ray, who asked me out for a movie date. Since they were identical twins, one never knew whether it was Roy or Ray that they were dating. Roy took me to the movie *Mr. Roberts* and Ray took me to a ball game. When I reported to my parents about my dates, my father was furious. He hated the Yankees and especially Mickey Mantle, who was never kind to the Orioles. He called Mr. McDaniel and told him to put a stop to my dating.

Another adventure occurred one day when the McDaniels planned a picnic on a little island in the middle of a pond on the farm. I had gone for a walk on the shore of the pond and Mr. McDaniel called out, "Watch out for the bull!"

I looked back and saw a bull in the distance but paid no attention until I heard a snort and there was the bull charging at me. I couldn't swim but jumped in the water and splashed my way to the island. I said to Mr. McDaniel, "I can't swim!"

He said, "You can now, honey."

Eventually the vacation ended, and we drove back to Baltimore.

A Working Life

I knew there was no money for college after graduating High School so, at seventeen, I got a job at the Chesapeake and Potomac Telephone Company in the steno pool. Ms. Werner was the head of it. She disliked me and vice versa. Mr. Chauncy Tatum was her superior and asked to have me sent for some of his work, to Ms. Werner's annoyance. He was an older man who also taught public relations at Johns Hopkins University. He suggested I come to one of his evening classes, which led to my taking several courses at the university. (My tuition was probably paid for by Uncle Bill).

When I was about twenty years old, I started dating a young man named Jack Phillips. He was a state trooper with the Maryland State Police. My father liked him and enjoyed the stories he had to tell. One of my father's favorites was when Jack was patrolling along a state highway and came upon a car pulled over on the berm. He shone his flashlight into the car and discovered an elderly couple in the back seat *in flagrante delicto*, as a Harvard lawyer would say. He suggested this was in inappropriate place for such activity, and the man said, "Son, at my age you have to take it when you can get it."

Jack left a ticket for illegal parking and departed without further disturbance.

Jack proposed to me one night with an engagement ring. My mother asked when we planned to get married. I said, "Oh, I can't marry him. I don't love him." She told me I had better let him know that and I should give back the engagement ring, which I did. He was disappointed but he was better off finding a wife who would love him.

Having had enough of Ms. Werner's hostility, I quit and started looking for a new job. I went to McCormick Tea, headquartered in Baltimore, but they wanted me to be a hostess in their tearoom, hoopskirt and all. I kept looking and found a secretarial position at Ham Brewing. Carleton Jones was in charge of public relations there, and he put me in the reception area. This led to decorative positions such as posing as Miss America on their float for the 4th of July parade. I didn't realize until later that my business success was partly due to my decorative qualities.

Schaefer Brewing, headquartered in New York City, later bought out Ham Brewing. Mr. Schaefer, my new boss, invited the secretarial staff to visit the New York headquarters. When his secretary left for a European vacation, he called and asked if I would come to New York while she was away, all expenses paid, of course. So I did and enjoyed the experience. Mr. Schaefer knew every one of his employees by name and would walk through the brewery, chatting with each person. He had kept everyone employed during Prohibition by making medical alcohol and was respected by all.

There was one memorable experience while I was at Schaefer Brewing. I didn't like beer and made no bones about it. So I was shocked one day when the brewmaster insisted that I come to a tasting. Despite my protests, I had to go. There were four unlabeled bottles and the participants were asked to rate each bottle on four qualities. I rated them all the same: stinky, bitter, sour, and smelly. The other judges carefully tasted each sample and gave their professional opinions in detailed descriptions. To my astonishment, the brewmaster announced that I was the winner. All four bottles were from the same batch. But I still don't like beer!

Chapter

4

My Life in Public Relations

F eeling that my future lay in public relations, I left Schaefer to go
work for Joseph Shaner Co., in Baltimore. There I met Carolyn
Taylor who became my best friend, and still is sixty years later. At the
time, she was working as a reporter for the *Baltimore Sun*. One day she
was told to interview Johnny Unitas, the world-famous quarterback.
She said, "What does he do?"

The editor must have had some misgivings.

After two years with Joseph Shaner Co., Mr. Shaner died and the
company closed. I then called Bob McCleary, the sales manager for
Schaefer Brewing. He was a big guy, standing at about six foot six.

"Do you still remember me?" I said.

"Of course."

"I hear you are hiring. Would you like to hire me?"

"Can you start next Monday?" So I did.

Mr. Schaefer had a to size replica of the *America*, the yacht that
won the first America's Cup race in 1951. Every detail was identical
to the original. Mickey McKinley was in charge of public relations
for Schaefer Brewing, and he invited me to join the crew for sailing
out of Annapolis. We did day trips from Annapolis to Newport

News. Some of the invited guests included the governor, mayors, newspaper publishers, and other dignitaries. On its maiden voyage, we sailed down the bay, where we met the *SS Homburg* on its maiden voyage from Germany. It made a large wake as we passed each other. A reporter from the *Baltimore Sun* was standing near the rail. He had enjoyed cocktail hour a little too long and, as we rolled in the wake of the *SS Homburg*, he fell overboard. Seated next to him was a sailing instructor from the Naval Academy who immediately threw the reporter a life buoy. I ran up to our captain, Jim Thorpe, and told him we had to back up. He said, "Sailboats can't back up!" To his disgust, he had to turn around and sail back to the man overboard. The reporter, now quite sober, was brought back aboard by a rope ladder.

Regular sailing made for a very enjoyable summer. It was annoying, and expensive, that the guests would help themselves to many engraved items on the ship. It was bad enough that we kept losing glasses, labels on bottles, and other engraved items. But the final straw was when someone wandered off the ship with the embroidered sheets from a bed.

Shortly after that summer, Schaefer Brewing decided to build a modern brewery in Allentown, Pennsylvania. I didn't want to move so they told me to apply for unemployment compensation, which they would support. I was so naïve. I said, "Oh, no, that's for poor people." They assured me it wasn't and, after the usual bureaucratic hassle, I began to receive weekly checks. I enjoyed sleeping in every morning, and when Carolyn had a vacation, we took off for England. We had a jolly time sightseeing and driving around the country. I didn't know how to drive a stick shift, so Carolyn did all the driving.

Chapter 5

Atapco

W hen I returned from England, I was directed to an employment agency, who sent me to an interview with American Trading and Production Corporation, also known as Atapco. I interviewed with Donald Statter, the director of Human Relations, and David Hirschorn, the company president. Hirschorn seemed to like me, but told me the company policy was to split the fee of the employment agency with the employee. I refused, saying I'd never paid that in any other job and wouldn't take the job if that were required. (What hutzpah!) After some arguing, he gave up and told Statter to forget the fee-splitting. I got the job and stayed with the Company for twenty-three years.

Before describing my years with Atapco, I should mention that I was dating a man named John Cooper. He was a pilot for Trans World Airlines (TWA), flying their big planes from the US to London or Paris. Before that, he had been a test pilot for McDonnell Douglas, but after a crash, he decided to move to a safer job. He was a few years older than me. We dated for five years or so, and we were in love. He was tall, dark, and handsome, and a great date. He took me to wonderful events, like the Kentucky Derby, and formal dances at the Ritz Carlton in New York. My father didn't care for him as he felt John belonged in a different social league than our family. We talked about marriage, but John was adamant that he did not want to have any children. I think he felt neglected by his wealthy family. I, on the other hand, wanted a large family. After much pondering, I decided marriage would be unfair to him, and to me, and we parted company. So much for my love life.

Back to my job: Atapco was an interesting company. It was a conglomerate owned by the Blaustein family with interests in oil and shipping, and had various production facilities. The Blaustein family were wealthy and generous contributors to many Baltimore charities. When the city was considering the development of the Harbor Front, Jacob Blaustein said, "I'll start it off with a modern twenty-eight story office building." Just what the developers wanted to hear. So Baltimore began its renewal.

The founder of the company, Louis Blaustein, had made his fortune in Oklahoma with American Oil, and oil drilling and production remained a part of Atapco. After Louis passed away, his son Jacob took the reins. He was highly regarded for his management skills. By the time I arrived, Morton Blaustein, a rather eccentric CEO, represented the third generation.

On my second day of employment in the personnel department, I got on the elevator and noticed a man in blue jeans and a plaid flannel shirt. He was out of place with the usual suit-and-tie crowd. As the elevator emptied, he turned to me and said, "Who are you? I don't know you."

I said, "I don't know you ether."

"Well, I'm Dr. Blaustein, and I own this company."

"I'm Marlene Herman, and I just started yesterday. I'm in personnel."

"Oh, so you work for Bob Statter. I'll get off on your floor and speak to him." And he did.

Mr. Statter was somewhat surprised to see his latest hire being escorted by Dr. Blaustein. He told Statter, "Marlene is a very attractive young lady and you look after her." I wasn't sure that this was the best way to start off with my new boss.

The Oil Division of Atapco was headquartered in Houston, Texas, and Calgary, Canada. I visited both places at various times on personnel matters. The Maritime Division was located in New York City, operated a fleet of tankers transporting oil, and manufactured products. A Real Estate Division that built and managed office buildings. Also, a company that made giftware, household items, and high tech electronic surveillance equipment. When Morton Blaustein wanted a particular carpet for a new building and the supplier didn't want to make it, he bought the carpet company and required them to make it.

At first, my duties were secretarial and as an interviewer for clerical positions. I would interview the applicant and give my recommendation to hire or not to the particular hiring manager. We occasionally disagreed. An example was an interview with a woman, Thelma, who was in her mid-fifties. We were looking for a switchboard operator. It was the old-fashioned plug-in-lines type, which Morton Blaustein insisted on because that is what his father had used. The interview included a typing test, which didn't make much sense because the position did not require much typing. I liked her and when I gave her the three-minute typing test, I let her go on for five minutes. When I took the application to Mr.

Warren Weiss, the hiring manager for this position, with my positive recommendation, he disagreed. "She's too old, and lives too far away and has to take a bus, so in bad weather she won't show up!"

I said give her a chance and we will see who's right. So, reluctantly, he did. A few weeks later, we had a big snowstorm. When I got to the office, Thelma was on the job taking telephone calls from all the employees saying they couldn't make it in. I took a list of all the employees who didn't make it in, pointing out that Mr. Weiss was late himself, but Thelma was on time. He came into my office and asked whether I preferred milk chocolate or dark chocolate. He left me with a Hershey's candy bar and the comment: "You were right."

Another experience didn't work out so well. I interviewed a woman who had quit her last job, which left me suspicious. But we hired her, which was a mistake. It was company policy to bring a doctor's excuse if you missed more than three days of work due to illness. This woman would regularly take off three days each week, claiming sickness. She always showed up on the fourth day. This went on for several weeks. Finally, I called her into my office (I had one by then!) and told her this was unsatisfactory. She was paid for five days of work a week, but only working two. I told her, the next time she took off work, she had to provide a doctor's excuse or she would be fired. I typed this out and made her sign it.

Sure enough, she continued to take off work, so I fired her. She filed a complaint with the state unemployment department. I went to the company's legal counsel to represent us at the hearing. He said they were too busy and I should go to represent the company myself. I objected that I didn't know anything about such hearings. He told me, "Do your best, good luck."

I went to the hearing and took with me all the records of her absences, plus the warning letter. The hearing examiner heard her complaint and asked if anyone was representing Atapco. "Yes, Your Honor, I am." I showed him the documents I brought and he denied her claim. After it was over, he asked if I would join him for lunch. I declined, as I had to get back to work. That ended my career as a trial lawyer, but with a perfect record.

By this time in my life, I had graduated to interviewing applicants for executive positions. I was still living at home. I mentioned to my mother that I was interviewing a man for the head of accounting. She said, "You don't know anything about accounting, how can you do that?" I told her I didn't have to. I could examine his credentials and references and, if they seemed okay, a senior manager would interview him.

My Modeling Career

One day, when I worked at Schaefer Brewing, the general manager invited me to lunch with a woman who modeled for department stores. She said I should consider modeling myself, as the pay is good and one got great discounts on clothes. I decided to try it and went to "modeling school" at Powers Modeling. The school taught me how to walk, how to sit, and general tips on model behavior. After that, I was hired to model for shows at Hutzler Brothers in Baltimore, and Woodward and Lothrop in Washington, D.C. The shows would be on weekday evenings and Saturdays. It was great and I was able to do this with my full-time job. The pay was anywhere from 15–50 dollars per hour, and you got to show off elegant clothes. My father had never been paid fifty dollars an hour and was shocked.

I was about five foot ten and assigned to "young sophisticated evening clothes" as one of the tallest models. I wore my hair in a French twist, with long earrings. In Washington, wives of senators, congressmen, and diplomats attended the shows. One time I got sick with strep throat. I had been fitted with clothes for the show, and the department head called to see if I couldn't come in, sick or not.

He said they didn't have another model that would fit the clothes. I could barely speak, but in a whisper, I told him I just couldn't do it. He had to postpone the show. That was enough to make me feel indispensable. I kept up my modeling career for another ten years.

Some of My Bosses

For my first decade or so at Atapco, my boss was Mr. Statter. His first name was Donald, but everyone called him Bob (his middle name was Robert). He was not a good boss, and I didn't like him. The feeling was mutual. He would summon me and another recruiter, Ray Borbridge, to his office and would just sit at his desk and stare out the window. Thinking great thoughts, we were led to believe. One day, while he was staring out the window, Ray crawled up on his desk on all fours and yelled "Bob!" Statter started in alarm, and I tried not to laugh.

Happily, a new boss arrived in the form of Paul McGillicuddy, vice president of Human Resources for all divisions of the company. He was Statter's boss and took over his corner office. He asked if I would like to be his secretary and I was delighted to say yes. So he told Statter to get a new secretary and invited me into his office to discuss my new position. He said he was here to help people learn, since he "knows everything." Making a joke out of it. He said if I made a mistake, to tell him about it. He might forgive me if I made the same mistake a second time, but if it happened a third time I would be fired. One thing he would not tolerate was anyone trying to undermine him. Since I readily accepted his conditions, he asked for a list of all the people in the department. He met with each one individually and gave them the same speech.

He was a great boss and gave me plenty of good advice. One year when I got a raise, he told me to put the difference in my 401(k) account each paycheck. I started to protest, but he said; "You've gotten along fine with your old salary, so you are going to save the addition. If you can't make it, I'll make up the difference. You will need it when you retire." I did as he directed.

As you might gather from his name, he was Irish and the biggest holiday for him was Saint Patrick's Day. He would arrange for the executives' private chef to serve an Irish menu. He would also invite people to his home for a great Irish feast. When my mother died, he asked if he could help with the funeral expenses, but I told him my thrifty family had taken care of it. To this day, I still get a card from him on Saint Patrick's Day. To have a wonderful friend like Paul McGillicuddy is one of life's blessings.

There were other interesting characters in our department too. One was an Englishman named Peter Downes, who handled insurance matters. He would arrive early every Monday morning and say, "Well, matey, any ships sunk, factories burned down, etc.?" I would find him with his feet up on my desk doing *The Times* (London) crossword puzzle. I'm not good at crossword puzzles, and *The Times* (London) one is completely mysterious. They just don't speak the same language as we do. But he would bring a cup of coffee and a bagel for me, which was a nice way to start the week.

My family had many friends at home as well. I lived with my parents the early years at Atapco. I have mentioned Paul and Catherine Wolinski (Uncle Paul and Aunt Cass) and their daughter,

Helen, who escorted me to school. Their other children were Earl and Herbert. Vera and Jimmy Means (Dr. Means) were long-time friends. Their daughter, Patty, was a close friend of mine. She later married Robert Forsythe (you will hear more of him later) and they had two daughters, Vera and Joyce. In their family, Vera was called Vera Lynn to distinguish her from her grandmother. Dr. Means treated many of my childhood ailments with good common sense. Another good friend was Jacqueline Boston. Her husband, Earl, was one of the sweetest, kindest men I have ever met, and he adored his wife. He was an officer in the Air National Guard.

Leaving Home

When I was thirty-five years old, I decided it was time for me to get my own apartment. I had been living with my parents all my life. I guess I wanted to assert my independence. I got an apartment in a complex in Towson called Glenmont. It was a nice "garden apartment" with a living room, dining room, den, bedroom, and kitchen. It had a balcony where I could sit outdoors and admire the gardens. My parents felt bad that they didn't have the money to send me to college, so they bought all the furniture for my apartment. I learned later that they grieved over my departure. Towson was an upscale suburban community northwest of Baltimore. It was about a thirty-five-minute drive to work, except at rush hour when it was twice as long.

My social life included friends from work and other people I knew. I dated several men, none of them memorable. Inez Treadwell, a friend from Atapco, and I went on a Caribbean cruise. The ship was the *Princess of the Cunard Line*.

During this period, I dated a man named Chuck Rohr. He was a few years older than me, and had his own business as a commercial artist. He designed for television commercials, magazines, and brochures. I liked him but he had a strange quality of not liking to go out around other people. He would take me to dinner and a movie, but wouldn't go to a baseball or football game. A party at somebody else's house was not allowed either. The breakup came when I wanted to go to a Christmas party at my friends, Jackie and Earl Boston's, house. I went by myself and met Jackie's boss, who invited me out to dinner and the symphony. Chuck was furious, and that was the final straw. We broke up. His mother, who I liked and who liked me, called me to get me to change my mind. Nope.

My father died in 1978, and I moved back to live with my mother. She was happy to have me back but felt she was imposing on me. I sold some of the apartment furniture, keeping special pieces Mom and I could use at home. I was sorry to lose my nice apartment, but I couldn't leave my seventy-year-old mother to live alone. Since Mom was my closest friend, I never regretted moving back.

But Mom died in 1993. I stayed on in the house for about a year, but then moved back to Towson.

Chapter 9

Back to Work

I n the early 1970s, I continued to climb up the corporate ladder and gain more responsibilities. After swearing to secrecy, I became responsible for entering pay increases for the executives. So I knew what everybody was paid. I noticed that top executives got free parking in the company garage while we peasants had to pay a monthly fee. I took this up with Dr. Blaustein one day. "It doesn't seem right that the people who could most afford the monthly fee don't have to pay it. Why don't you make parking free for everybody?"

He considered this, but said, "No, they won't appreciate it if it's free." However, he agreed to cut the monthly fee in half. A small victory for the working stiffs.

I had my own office and a secretary. Elva was an old maid and a bit fussy, but a good worker. One day she came into my office clutching her pocketbook. I thought it was strange that the pocketbook didn't leave her side all day, and I finally asked her why.

She said, "Because I'm buying a car this evening and I'm carrying the cash to buy it." I was a bit alarmed and asked her how much cash she was carrying. "Twenty-two thousand dollars."

I said, "You took the bus to work and walked several blocks carrying all that money? How are you going to get to the car dealer?" When she said her nephew was going to pick her up, I went out and stood at the curb with her, looking around anxiously until he arrived. When time came to pay for the car, she dumped all the money on the salesperson's desk. Dumbfounded, he didn't know what to do. So he called all the people working there, and they locked the doors to keep anyone from entering. Then they spent an hour or so counting and recounting the money.

One summer day, in the 1970s, Helen Ritter, Aunt Cass's daughter, previously Helen Wolinski, came into town to have lunch with me. We ate outdoors at Harbor Place. We looked at the new Baltimore World Trade Center, which was still under construction. The exterior was finished, and they were currently doing the interior. Helen said she wished she could see what the view was like from the top floor, so I said, "Let's go have a look."

She said, "They won't let us in."

I took that as a challenge. "Follow me!"

There was a guard seated at a desk inside, so I walked up to him and read his name badge. I said, "Kevin, how have you been? How's the family?" A good subject for an older man. He beamed and told me about his grandchildren. I then asked, "How are the boys coming on the top floor?"

"Just great, they have been working hard."

I said, "They should be, considering what we're paying them." He laughed and said he would get an elevator for us.

We took the elevator, Helen worrying we would be arrested. When we got to the top, I flashed the boss sitting at a desk my parking pass. He didn't bother to look at it; instead, he was looking at us. "How are you coming along?" I asked.

"They are working hard."

I tried the same line. "They should be, considering what we pay them." I then told him I needed to write a report. He told us to look around. I took Helen to the various sides and pointed out the sights of the city, including Fort McHenry, of The Star-Spangled Banner fame, out in the harbor. Helen studiously took notes.

One of the workers came up and said he had a five-dollar bet with his buddy. He said we would install red carpet and his buddy said no, I told him that he lost. "I don't want people to be distracted by bright colors when they get off the elevator. I want them to look out the windows instead."

We continued our "inspection" and he came back with another bet. His buddy bet we would put drapes on the windows. I told him he had just won back his five bucks. "I want people to look at the view, not the drapes."

We walked over to a raised section that had a picture of Jacob Blaustein and other memorabilia celebrating his leadership of the harbor restoration. Back at the ground floor, I wished Kevin well and asked how old his grandchildren were. That brought out photos before he said, "Come back soon!"

The building was finally finished in 1977 and continues to be the show place of the harbor. It has an outside viewing platform on the 27th floor. It is angled so that that one corner looks like it is rising out of the harbor. The lights on the outside focus on parabolic mirrors that shine out over the water. Sailors have told me they can see the lights up to ten miles away. It is Baltimore's lighthouse. When I visited later, I was pleased to see that the carpet on the 30th floor was a soft blue-green and there were no drapes. They followed my advice!

A few stories about my rather eccentric employer, Morton Blaustein. He had been somewhat spoiled as a child. As an example, when his father asked him what he was going to write for his senior college thesis, Morton told him it would be how to drill an oil well. His father said, "You don't know how to drill an oil well. Come down to Houston and we will drill an oil well." He did and got a good grade for his thesis.

When his secretary needed a new assistant, I interviewed a woman who seemed qualified, but I warned her that her boss could be rather difficult at times. She said to try her out; she could handle him. On her first day, he wrote a check for five hundred dollars and told her to take it down to his bank and bring back four hundreds and two fifties. She did and put the money on his desk. He shouted a horrified, "*Ew!*"

She thought he might be having a stroke. When asked what the matter was, he shouted, "*It's soiled currency!*" She was sent back to the bank and told the manager the money was for Dr. Blaustein and it had to be clean money. She learned.

He remarried, and the new Mrs. Blaustein did not put up with his sloppy attire. He was sent to a tailor and, after, would show up wearing a beautiful suit, shirt, and tie. He complained to me that the suit had only one pair of pants, and his off the rack suits had two.

But he could be generous with the charities he favored. Once he sent me down to get a company check for $250,000 to send to Israel, supposedly for planting trees. I wondered how it was really spent. When the President of Johns Hopkins University visited him, he would send him home with a similarly large contribution.

When interviewing applicants, it is sometimes difficult to get the information one needs. We had an applicant for a job in accounting that required a CPA qualification. I checked his college credentials, which were satisfactory, and asked about his previous employment. He had worked for the FBI for seven years. I asked him what his job had been. He said it was confidential and he wasn't allowed to tell me. I called the FBI and got the right person there to confirm that he had been employed there. Then I asked what his job had been, and the FBI representative said she wasn't allowed to tell me. She couldn't verify his salary either, but she said I could tell her what salary I would be offering. I gave her the number and she said, "Wow! That's a good salary for custodial work."

That's all I needed to hear. I sent him the form rejection letter, but he came in and asked why he had been turned down. I said, "Because you lied to me." He shrugged his shoulders and said it had been worth a try.

Occasionally you can help someone along their way. I sometimes went to local schools and talked to students about job opportunities when they graduated. I went to a schoolroom one morning and the place was chaos. The teacher was a young man with a tired shirt, no tie or coat, and in need of a haircut. The students weren't paying attention to him. I told him he was a disgrace as a teacher and had no business teaching. He agreed and said he had no qualifications for teaching. He had graduated from college with an accounting degree, but he couldn't get a job, so he took this teaching job just to pay the rent. We had no openings in accounting at that time, but I had gotten to know other personnel people in large firms. I checked around to see if they had any openings in accounting. My counterpart at

Baltimore Gas and Electric said she did, so I called the teacher and told him to check it out.

About six months later, the young man showed up in my office wearing a suit and tie and carrying a briefcase. He told me he not only got the job, but after six months, he had been promoted to a higher position and he wanted to thank me. I wished him well and felt a little proud of myself.

I would often be called to Dr. Blaustein's office for meetings or to deal with various problems. One day, his secretary called and said, "Marlene, come up here. I have something to show you!" I did, and she opened a large box that contained the most gorgeous fur coat I had ever seen. It was from Neiman Marcus, and it was a present for Mrs. Blaustein. It was a Russian black sable fur coat and the price tag said $245,000! She said, "Take it out, Dr. Blaustein is busy and won't be out for some time." I lifted it carefully and just then, Dr. Blaustein popped out of his office.

He said, "Oh, Marlene, isn't it lovely. Try it on! They will put my wife's initials on it. Where should I have them located?"

I tried it on and never felt anything so luxurious. I looked pretty good in it; after all I was a model. I told him they would have to cut the coat because Mrs. Blaustein was about eight inches shorter me. "And then she should decide where the initials go." I decided.

I regretted the loss of all that beautiful fur when they cut it. He said they would fly over to fit the coat without charge. I thought that, at that price, they could afford to fly over several times.

Another memorable occasion involved the Marine Division. I got a call one day from the captain of the *American Trader*, the company's largest ship. Why would he want to talk to me? He said he was two days out from Hong Kong Harbor and it was essential that the ship be met at the dock by the Brink's truck with paychecks in cash for the crew. It was the end of their voyage and they were always paid at the end of their six months at sea. The payroll was about $2 million. "If they don't get the cash the minute they step off the ship there will be a riot." He explained.

I asked why he was calling me. I didn't have anything to do with payroll. He said the word in the company was, if you wanted to get something done, you called Marlene. I trotted down to the payroll officer's office. He said he had already wired the funds and they should be there. I suggested he call the bank in Hong Kong, which he did, and they said they hadn't received the funds. He sent the funds a second time. Mission accomplished, I thought.

The next day, I was in a meeting with several people in Dr. Blaustein's office. There was a timid knock on the door, which was met with an outraged shout of *come in* from Dr. Blaustein. (He hated to be interrupted.) In came my secretary, Elva, trembling. She and said the captain of the *American Trader* called and said, "I am one day out from Hong Kong Harbor and the *(expletives deleted)* payroll still isn't there! If it's not there tomorrow morning I am going to sink the *(expletives deleted)* ship in Hong Kong Harbor!"

Alarmed, Dr. Blaustein said, "Marlene, you better go and take care of this!"

So I scurried back to the payroll officer, who said he had sent the funds twice. I told him he had better try a third time. He did. The funds arrived in time, and the ship didn't sink. It took several weeks to straighten out the missing wired funds.

Well, all things come to an end, and on the death of Morton Blaustein the family decided to downsize the company. They wanted the cash. The president's nephew, Louis Thalheimir, took over his position. They began first by selling the Marine Division, followed by the other divisions, leaving only the real estate and oil and gas divisions. They no longer needed a personnel department, so I was terminated along with the others. I was fifty-two years old at the time, and I complained to Louis that if I didn't stay until I was fifty-five, I would lose my pension and health benefits. After pondering this, he said, "It's simple. We just have to keep you on the payroll until you are fifty-five. I can't promise any increases, however. And you can't come into the office."

With this unusual promise, I packed up my desk and left the building forever. And yes, for three more years I received my paychecks twice a month and my pension and health insurance ever since. A strange, but generous, arrangement for which I am grateful.

A New Life

After my mother died the next year, my friend, Carolyn, now Mrs. Gutierrez, advised me to sell the house. The neighborhood was changing and not for the better. I got the same advice from Bob and Patty Forsythe, who now lived in Pennsylvania. Reluctantly, I followed their advice and sold the house that I had lived in nearly all my life. I bought a fifth-floor condominium in a complex named Towson Gate in Towson. I had a balcony that looked out over a courtyard. Two bedrooms, a dining room, kitchen, and a storage area containing the washer and dryer. It also had floor to ceiling shelves, perfect for appliances, seasonal decorations, etc. I liked my new digs.

A new turn in my life began with my friend, Patty Forsythe, and her mother Vera Means. Patty was a few years ahead of me in school. Robert Forsythe, known as Bob, and Patty were married after he graduated from the University of Maryland. He became a salesperson, working for Geigy Pharmaceutical, a Swiss company now called Ciba-Geigy. He was a born salesperson and progressed well, but in the mid-1960s, he decided that this was not how he wanted to spend his life. He enrolled in Pittsburgh Theological Seminary and moved his family, which now included daughters Vera Lynn and Joyce, to live in an old Victorian house on campus. On his graduation from the seminary, he began his career as a Presbyterian pastor in Midway, a small town in Washington County, Pennsylvania. He later served as a pastor in various Pennsylvania towns before becoming the pastor of Riverview Presbyterian Church in Pittsburgh. The church was near the Byzantine Seminary, and when he went to visit its faculty he was persuaded to teach a course there, which he did for twenty-one years.

Enough about Bob. My friend Patty was diagnosed with breast cancer, and after the usual treatment and chemotherapy, she succumbed to the dreaded disease in 2001. Before she died, she made me promise I would be with her before she passed. While living in Baltimore, I got the call in February to come immediately. I was being treated for a leg injury and the doctor told me I should not drive to Pittsburgh. He didn't approve of flying either, but it was the better choice, and I did it. I got there in time, held her hand, and talked to her. She died a few hours later that night.

Life had gotten a bit lonesome with most of my family and friends no longer with me. But Bob Forsythe came to Baltimore several times that year, accompanied by our mutual friend Judy Lytle, for the sake of propriety. Later in the year, they were visiting and were about to return to Pittsburgh when I mentioned that I was going to the dentist the next day for some painful surgery. He said they would stay to take me and then bring me home. That was welcome because I was still groggy from the surgery when it was time to go home. At my home, Bob said, "I love you Marlene, and we should get married. Will you marry me?" In my groggy state, I mumbled something about thinking about it.

During the night, my dreams were rather puzzling, and when I got up the next morning, I didn't know whether Bob had proposed or whether I had dreamed it. So I was quiet at breakfast until Bob said, "What's your answer?"

I said I would think about it, which I did for about a month. I concluded that I would like to marry him, and the first person I talked to was my friend and minister, Joe Skillman. He was delighted and lifted me off my feet, which is no small undertaking. He told me there was nothing left for me in Baltimore. My family was gone, and I was no longer working. He also said he would come to the wedding. I pointed out that it would be in Pittsburgh in the winter, but he reminded me that he had spent winters in Buffalo and had no fear of snow.

The big event was on January 18, 2002 at Old St. Luke's Church, along Chartiers Creek, west of Pittsburgh. Carolyn was my bridesmaid, Joe Skillman gave me my vows, and Jorge Gutierrez, Carolyn's husband and an Episcopal priest, did the communion part of the service. Don Bolls, a Presbyterian minister and friend of Bob's, gave him his vows. Of course, Bob's daughters, Vera Lynn and Joyce, were there, along with husband Rick Purcell and their children Evan and Joyce. We had a delightful dinner for everyone at Lamont, a restaurant in the Mount Washington neighborhood in Pittsburgh, with fine views of the city and its rivers. Bob had many friends, so there were fifty or so guests present.

We spent our honeymoon at the Nemacolin resort in the mountains southeast of Pittsburgh. There was a heavy snowstorm, resulting in closed roads. That didn't matter to us honeymooners though.

We bought a condominium town house in Wexford. It had three stories, with a patio at the first level and a deck over it, off the dining room. Bob had retired from the ministry to take care of Patty, but the Presbytery persuaded him to take a temporary post at a small church next to Old St. Luke's called Chartiers Valley Presbyterian Church. The congregation had shrunk to about a dozen people and his duty was to close the church. The typical congregation showed up for the first Sunday, but the following Sunday there were twice as many. The congregation continued to grow each Sunday until there were eighty or more attending. They were not interested in closing the church and got busy rehabbing the building. They were not a wealthy congregation but they were willing to work hard. We enjoyed the whole process, and I contributed with my decorating ideas. Bob had refused to take a salary, but the Presbytery couldn't approve that, so the church paid a salary, which he gave back to the church, satisfying the Presbytery and the IRS.

He was at home in the pulpit, and his style was informal and interesting. He didn't hesitate to make remarks about his wife, sometimes to my annoyance. One Sunday I dozed off and he said, "Would someone wake up Marlene?" Much to the amusement of everybody in the congregation, except me.

We liked our home in Wexford, but it was on three levels with a lot of steps. One day, when Bob was ill, I carried a tray of food up to him and said, "Someday we won't be able to handle these stairs. We should look for a home without stairs." He agreed, and after searching, we found a home in Hampton Township, in northern Allegheny County. The living quarters were all on the first floor, no basement, with a guest bedroom and storage closets on the second floor. There was a nice yard, and a community swimming pool nearby. There was also a large Catholic church nearby called St. Catherine of Sweden.

A day came when Bob had to have a knee replacement at Passavant Hospital. He went to a rehab facility after the surgery. When he was recuperating, a friend from the past visited him. An attorney named Robert Patton had served with him on the Presbytery Board of Trustees, but they had lost track of each other. But, Vera Lynn Purcell, Bob's daughter, sang in a church choir with Patton. Knowing of their past friendship, she asked him to visit her father at the rehab facility because he was bored to death. So Patton came to visit him one Saturday morning when I happened to be there. I was tired and not very interested in the reminiscences of two elderly men. They chatted happily for quite a while and, when Patton was leaving, he suggested that he and his wife would be happy to come and have lunch with us when Bob had recovered. One might think, when fate has something in store for a person, there would be a little nudge or something. But, no, I didn't realize this moment would become important to my future.

A few weeks later, Patton called and we met him and his wife, Ginnie, at our favorite restaurant, Carmodies. Ginnie was an attractive woman and mother of four. She had been diagnosed with ovarian cancer and was undergoing chemotherapy. The two of us enjoyed talking when we could get a word in over the two voluble men. When the Pattons were leaving, Robert said, "Forsythe, I should have guessed you would have a beautiful wife."

After they left, Bob said to me, "Do you think he was hitting on you?" I told him some people are just trying to be polite.

I think we had lunch one or two more times with the Pattons that summer. But summer led to autumn, and to a day I hate to remember, the worst day of my life, but I must relate it. During that thanksgiving weekend, we went shopping on Route 19. As we left the store, we pulled out onto the four-lane highway. An SUV coming at high speed hit our car, demolishing it. Bob was killed instantly. I was carried off in an ambulance to Allegheny General Hospital with broken bones and multiple other injuries. I hate to recall this and the weeks that followed. I could not attend Bob's funeral, as I was confined to my bed. Joe Skillman and his wife Barb came and stayed with me during the funeral. The funeral was at Northmont Presbyterian Church, where Bob had served as a pastor. I understand the church was overflowing, with twelve ministers and priests participating. I later learned that one of the many in the congregation was Robert Patton.

Starting Over

At Allegheny General, after the accident, Dr. Swieki, a handsome young man, examined me. He told me surgery would be required for my broken ankle bones, and it would be best if they started immediately. I said I wanted to think about it, so he said he would be back in twenty minutes. My friend, Charlotte Stevenson, was in the room with me, and said she didn't think I had any choice but to have the surgery. So I agreed and was whisked off to the operating room. From then on, I was mostly unconscious during my hospital stay. However, after six days I was discharged from the hospital wearing a heavy boot to protect my ankle.

I spent several months recuperating from the accident. My stepdaughter, Joyce, and friend, Judy Lytle, moved in to take care of me. My other stepdaughter, Vera Lynn, who had a long drive from Mt. Lebanon, visited us regularly. By springtime, I was able to move around and could sit outside on sunny days.

Life goes on, even when you're grieving. We got through Christmas. My late husband, Bob, and I had put up the tree and decorated it before the accident. Vera Lynn and the Purcell family came, brought Christmas dinner, and did the same for New Year's

Eve. We were a sorry lot and lacked the usual wishes for a happy New Year.

In the New Year, I consulted an attorney at Buchanan Ingersoll about a lawsuit for the accident. They didn't do automobile accidents, but recommended the firm of Goldberg, Kamin, and Garvin. They accepted the case on a contingent fee basis, as is typical. My case was assigned to John Arminas, a young associate. He began the process by hiring an expert witness. There were no witnesses to the accident, so the testimonies would come from the expert and me. One might think that all one has to do is file a complaint and go to trial, but one would be wrong. The wheels of justice grind fine but they grind exceedingly slow is, apparently, a common saying among lawyers.

The rest of the year passed without any remarkable events. I gradually healed, and the holidays were not quite as depressing as the previous year.

On New Year's Day, Rick was playing at the Duquesne Club, and Vera Lynn and Joyce took me to the 4:30 seating. As we were leaving, we met Robert Patton, who also went by Bob, coming into the club for the later seating. Ginnie Patton had died the previous year, leaving Bob a widower. There were the usual New Year's greetings and Bob said to me, "Marlene, why don't we have lunch one of these days?"

I said I would like that, and Vera Lynn said she would too. Bob said, "Not you, Vera."

So he wanted to have lunch with just me. This caused a certain amount of gossip as we were leaving, which finally annoyed Joyce, and she said, "He will call, and she will go. Can we talk about something else?"

He did call a few days later, and we went to a nice lunch at the restaurant at Hartwood Acres. We both enjoyed it, a break from a lonely time for both of us. He took me home and asked me if I would like to go on a real date: a movie, and dinner afterward. I was happy to say yes. That date led to many more. Dinners at the Duquesne Club, concerts at the Pittsburgh Symphony and Pittsburgh Opera, and more. Bob was disappointed when I told him I didn't care for opera music, as he loved opera and had been on the board of Pittsburgh Opera for many years. So I'm not perfect!

One night, I had a vivid dream that I clearly remembered when I woke up. In my dream, the doorbell rang and I opened the door to find a man in a trench coat standing there. He showed me his badge and said, "I'm from the IRS. May I come in?"

I let him in and said, "I have paid my taxes!"

He said, "Yes, we know. This is about the taxes on $90 million that Mr. Patton owes."

I said, "I can't pay the taxes on $90 million!"

He said, "Ma'am, you have to bring something to the table." That was the end of the dream.

Bob was coming over for lunch that day, and I couldn't wait to tell him about my dream. I called him on his cell phone while he was en route. I told him we had never discussed money and then I described my dream. There was a brief pause, and then he said, "Thank God, they didn't find the Cayman account." I have been trying to find out the password to the "Cayman account" ever since, without success.

One nice spring day, I was invited to a cookout at Bob's daughter, Laura Norton's, home. The occasion was to celebrate Tommy Norton's high school graduation. The Nortons had a nice home in

Peters Township, Washington County. Susan Altman, Bob's middle daughter, and her husband, Dan, were there. Bob's son, Tom, was also there. He lived near Freedom, Pennsylvania. Bob's daughter Barbara, the oldest of his daughters, lived in Farmville, Virginia with her husband, Niels Kiewiet de Jonge. They were not at Laura's but called. Each of Bob's four children had three children of their own, for a total of twelve grandchildren. Wow! I always wished for a big family.

Obviously, our relationship had become serious, but Bob told me we could not discuss marriage, much less getting engaged, before my lawsuit was tried or settled. He said it would limit any claim for damages and certainly would not make my lawyer happy. He said we wouldn't even talk about it, because I would be deposed and questioned about any such relationship. He said, "You would not be a good liar on cross." So the subject was taboo.

Bob's daughters expressed some concern to him about his getting married so soon after Ginnie's death (it had only been a year). He gathered all his children together at the wedding of his grandson, Erik, and told them they did not need to worry, as marriage was out of the question while the litigation continued. He said, "I will tell you when you need to start worrying." That seemed to put an end to their concerns, at least for the time being.

I was concerned about the apparent lack of progress in the litigation. Bob suggested that he could accompany me when I went to meet with my lawyer. A meeting was scheduled and we went to see John Arminas together. Bob explained he was "just a friend of the family" who was trying to help me understand the process. Even though he had been a member of the bar for fifty years, he was not giving me any legal advice, and would not have been competent to do so, as his practice did not involve personal injury cases.

John, who explained he was waiting to get the expert's report, had not filed the complaint yet. Bob asked what the statute of limitations was. (He knew damn well it was two years.) John assured him we had plenty of time. Bob told him that his senior partner, John Buchanan, always said to their young lawyers, "Fear nothing but God and the statute of limitations."

The meeting ended and, when we were leaving, John's senior partners stopped Bob. They knew him as the managing partner of Buchanan Ingersoll, and were quite curious about what he was doing at their office. They had a friendly chat and John Arminas learned that someone was watching over his shoulder.

The complaint was filed shortly after that and, as predicted, I was scheduled for a deposition by opposing counsel. It was not a pleasant experience, as the opposition's lawyer was rude and obnoxious. Also, as predicted, he wanted to know about my personal life.

"Are you seeing anyone?" he questioned me.

"Yes. I see a number of my friends."

"Are you romantically involved with anyone? Are you sleeping with anyone?" I got indignant, told him I was a widow of a Presbyterian minister, and found his questions obnoxious. He said, "Just answer the question."

I was upset after this and complained to Bob about the lawyer's rude behavior. He just laughed and said the lawyer was doing just what he intended to do: see if I could be upset as a witness while letting me know that a trial would be unenjoyable. After that, my lawyer deposed the defendant, who had killed my husband. When asked if he had tried to brake, the man said he had. My lawyer pointed out that the black box in his truck showed that he had not. The case was scheduled for trial, but we would wait for several months.

Eventually, settlement negotiations began. We refused the first offer, but we accepted the revised offer and the litigation was over!

Now we could talk about the unthinkable: marriage! No dramatic groom getting down on one knee offering an engagement ring. Nope. His romantic proposal was, "Well, when are we going to do this?"

Lawyer Patton said we had to see his attorney and former partner, John Schmerling, to prepare a prenuptial agreement. I didn't know why we needed this, but he was right. If neither of us was around, we didn't want the two families to have any disputes. John said he couldn't represent me, so he suggested a lawyer in another firm. It was all done promptly, with full disclosure of each of our assets, but I didn't find any $90 million account or a bank account in the Caymans. Darn.

After the prenup was signed, I invited my former stepdaughters, Vera Lynn and Joyce, for lunch and told them Bob had asked me to marry him and I said yes. It was greeted with enthusiasm by Vera Lynn, but with some sadness from Joyce, who was going to lose her North Hills neighbor.

My unromantic groom also refused to choose an engagement ring. We went to a jeweler recommended by Vera Lynn, Robert Truver, together and I chose a nice engagement ring. It had a sapphire surrounded by small diamonds. We also chose simple gold wedding rings. By then, Bob's children had gotten to know me and they were enthusiastic about the wedding. The only warning from them was no givebacks!

The great day arrived on July 22, 2012, at 4:00 p.m. Our wedding was in the chapel of Southminster Presbyterian Church with Reverend Dan Merry, Bob's pastor, presiding. Guests were limited to family and a few close friends. Carolyn was my maid of honor and Tom, Bob's son, was his best man. Following the I dos, the assembly adjourned to a room at the Duquesne Club for the celebration dinner. What a happy time for everyone there! The children and grandchildren occasionally reminded of the "no givebacks" rule, but everyone was in a jubilant mood. We spent our wedding night at the Fairmont Hotel, where Carolyn and Jorge were also staying. We breakfasted with them and delivered them to the airport to return to Massachusetts.

Our home in Providence Point had been undergoing renovations before we married. It is a patio home with a living room, dining room, kitchen, den, and two bedrooms, each with a bath. It has ample room for two people. I was given the decorating decision-making power. Bob's furniture that we didn't keep was distributed to his four children or given away. The kids chose which pieces they would accept and a moving van came and hauled them away: three stops in Pennsylvania and one in Virginia. I called a painter I knew who came, painted the whole house interior, and installed some ceiling moldings. I have continued to renovate or replace items in the succeeding years. Home decorating is my favorite occupation and it's a shame I didn't choose to do this as my profession.

After the wedding, we returned to our new home. I became acquainted with the residents of Providence Point and the members of Southminster Presbyterian Church, where Bob still sings in the choir.

Chapter 12

The Traveling Pattons

B efore we were married, I was warned that people born under the zodiac sign of Sagittarius loved to travel. Both Bob and Ginnie were Sagittarians and had traveled throughout the United States, Canada, and many other countries throughout the world. The warning was proven correct, as we have spent part of each year (except for COVID-19 years) traveling. Bob finally got to his 50th state, North Dakota, and to his fifth continent, South America, after we were married.

Before we were married, we went on a Caribbean cruise in 2011 with people from Providence Point. We had separate rooms for the sake of propriety, but they were connected. That same year, we were invited by Vera Lynn to join her and Rick on a Howard Hanna trip to Prague in the Czech Republic. The Hannas have an annual trip for their top sales agents, and Vera Lynn is always included. The trips include lavish entertainment and first-class traveling. They were happy to include us but, of course, we paid our own way. Hoddy Hanna and Bob are old friends. We loved Prague and have visited since.

IN 2012, we went on what we called our honeymoon trip, flying to London first, where we stayed at the Royal Automobile Club, which has reciprocity with the Duquesne Club. It was a rather rainy visit, but we saw Kensington Palace and went to a delightful English comedy called *Yes, Prime Minister.* Following London, we went to Budapest, a fascinating city, where we embarked on an AMA Waterways cruise on the Danube. After spending several days in Budapest, the cruise proceeded upriver to Vienna. We didn't have enough time in Vienna to enjoy it fully, so we would like to go back sometime. The cruise proceeded into Germany, where we made several stops, finally finishing in Nuremburg. Let me show you some of our photos!

In 2013, we went off on another Howard Hanna trip to the Portuguese Madeira Islands. I believe the largest one is named Madeira. These are beautiful volcanic islands, rising steeply from the sea. They are parallel to Casablanca, Morocco, in Africa. Thus, a pleasant warm vacation spot in late winter. We had the usual jolly time with the real estate agents, especially Vera Lynn and Rick, and the trip concluded in Lisbon.

The next big trip was in 2014, when we took the Rocky Mountaineer trip on Canadian Railways in early autumn. First, we traveled across the US on Amtrak, going to the Grand Canyon. Bob had been there twice before, but it was the first time for me. The sight of the canyon was so beautiful it brought me to tears. We then flew from Los Angeles to Vancouver, where the Rocky Mountaineer tour started. The mountain scenery was breathtaking, and I would do it again if the opportunity ever arises. The beautiful scenic railway cars, staying overnight in fine hotels. Our baggage would be left in our room when we would leave one stop and would magically appear in our new room at the next stop. We made stops in Banff, Lake Louise, Jasper, and then we circled back to Vancouver. I recommend this trip for everyone.

That year, we also visited our friends, Jon and Carol Walton, in Naples, Florida. They have a lovely apartment with views of the Gulf.

We liked to take spring trips to Williamsburg, Virginia and stay at the Inn. One evening, Bob went to the bar at the Inn. He sat at the end seat and there was another woman sitting not too far away, rather dripping with gold jewelry. I asked if he had tried to pick her up. He said he didn't know how to pick up a woman at a bar. "Let's practice." I said, "Do you come here often?"

He replied, "Yes, I keep a room here for when I'm passing through. My pilot flew me up here from Florida. I recently lost my wife, and I'm on my way to Cape Cod. I don't know whether to sell it though."

I expressed sympathy for his loss. The other woman moved up closer to hear this. He said, "I was going to have dinner with my pilot, but I don't know when he will get through golfing. Are you free to join me?" I told him I would be pleased to and we left.

The next evening, we went back to the bar. The woman, still dripping with gold, was there waiting. I said to her, "Did you have a nice day?"

She said, "I'm sure you did."

We still laugh about his educational experience.

In 2015, Bob went to Argentina with the Norton family. His granddaughter, Julia, was planning to learn Spanish to become a bilingual speech therapist. She went to Buenos Aires for a course in Spanish and was fortunate enough to live with a retired couple who treated her like their own granddaughter. Bob and the Norton family had a great visit and, after Buenos Aires, flew to the Iguazu National Park, home of the great Iguazu Falls. When Eleanor Roosevelt visited, she said, "Poor, Niagara."

They went on to Rio de Janeiro and stayed in Copacabana. All in all, it was a memorable trip for everyone. I decided not to go on this trip, as I might slow everybody down, but I am glad Bob went and everyone had a joyous trip.

We did make what has become an annual trip with Vera Lynn, Rick, and Joyce to Kiawah Island near Charleston, South Carolina. We stay at The Sanctuary resort. We enjoyed swimming in the Atlantic and the swimming pools at the resort. We usually had dinner at the famous golf club there too.

In 2016, we went with Barbara and Niels to Amsterdam where we stayed at a bed-and-breakfast for several nights. Amsterdam is our favorite city in Europe. Besides sightseeing, we visited Niels's cousins who live there. We were impressed with this fine family and their hospitality.

From Amsterdam, we took the train to Rotterdam where we boarded the Holland America ship *S.S. Rotterdam*. This was for a memorable transatlantic voyage to Boston. We had stops in Bergen, Norway; the Shetland Islands off Northern Scotland; and Iceland, where we crossed the arctic circle and had several stops with the last being in Reykyavic. What a fascinating country. Next was on to two small towns in Greenland. Then the rest of the way to North America, landing in St. John's, Newfoundland. Finally, we sailed into Boston Harbor, and then the flight home. What a voyage!

If that wasn't enough travel that year, we also took an AMA Waterways cruise down the Rhine into Switzerland. These river cruises are a very relaxing way to travel. In addition to the one I mentioned on the Danube, we also had a river cruise in Holland and another one in Belgium.

In 2017, we stayed home, that is, in the United States. We took trips to the Nortons' vacation home in Rock Lake, Ohio, and to Cape Cod. Alas, while there I ended up in the hospital with a gallbladder attack. Turns out, I was passing a gallstone. After several days in the hospital, I was told I needed to have my gallbladder removed. I elected to return to Pittsburgh for that the surgery. I had the good fortune to have Dr. Steven Evans as my surgeon. He became a good friend, and we went on a Caribbean cruise with him, Vera Lynn, and Rick in 2018.

In February 2018, we went to Naples, Florida, to a resort where Marty and Flo Richman also stayed. Marty was one of Bob's classmates from Harvard Law School and both were on the Law Review. Marty practiced in New York, and ended up in the K&L Gates office in New York. He was one of Bob's daughter Susan's partners. Small world.

In 2019, Bob finally got to visit his 50th state, North Dakota, with his son Tom. They flew to Bismarck, and then drove to the Theodore Roosevelt National Park in the Badlands. He told me the Badlands are beautiful and I took his word for it.

In 2020, we went for what has proven to be our last cruise to the Caribbean. We disembarked to find that another cruise ship in the West Coast was under quarantine because of COVID-19. We had escaped just in time. The pandemic has put an end to our travels, at least for the time being.

Family Matters

One might think, from the preceding chapter, that we spent all our time traveling, but that was not so. Most of our time was spent in our happy home in Providence Point, enjoying friends and family. As if four children and twelve grandchildren weren't enough for the Patton family, the great-grandchildren began to appear. Wylie Murdoch was the first to arrive, in 2012. We visited him and his mother, Devon, at Magee Hospital. As we were leaving, we heard him crying. Bob said, "Good lungs." He was followed by a second great-grandson, Mac, in 2013. The third Murdoch, Lem, arrived in 2016.

The Erik KdJ family gave us our first great-granddaughter, Louisa, in 2014, followed by another great-grandson, Alexander, in 2016. Vivienne, Erik's second daughter, was born in 2019.

Brittany and Aaron Berman had their first daughter, Landon, in 2017. She was joined another great-grandchild, Daphne, in 2021. Both girls were skiing by the time they turned two.

Chad and Audra KdJ had their first daughter, Flora, in 2018. Chad and Audra had another daughter, Gray, in 2021.

Bob's daughter Laura became a grandma in 2020 with the arrival of Adam Patterson, son of Kevin and Emily. They moved to Grand Rapids, Minnesota, and Grandma Laura couldn't stand be separated from Adam, so she and Chris moved there too.

Daphne joined her sister Flora in 2021.

There we have the great-grandchildren so far, but we hear that others may be on the way. Stay tuned. Bob is hoping for twenty-four of them. I held most of these infants soon after they were born, and they are the dearest little babies one has ever seen.

We continue to enjoy life with our friends at Providence Point. I had Christmas parties every year until COVID-19 prohibited it, with thirty some people attending each year. The staff at Providence Point provided the food and a bartender. We are hopeful that this Christmas, 2021, will allow us to resume. We usually eat at the Neville Room, and sometimes friends join us. Bill and Linda Dempsey, Mike and Mickey Tehan, Lois Singleton, and Vonnie Marshall are frequent dinner companions. I won't list everybody, so don't be offended if I haven't mentioned you.

Conclusion

No life is unmitigated pleasure or sorrow. I feel balanced. I have been most fortunate in my life, and I hope to enjoy it with friends and family for a few more years.

Printed in the United States
by Baker & Taylor Publisher Services